CONTENTS

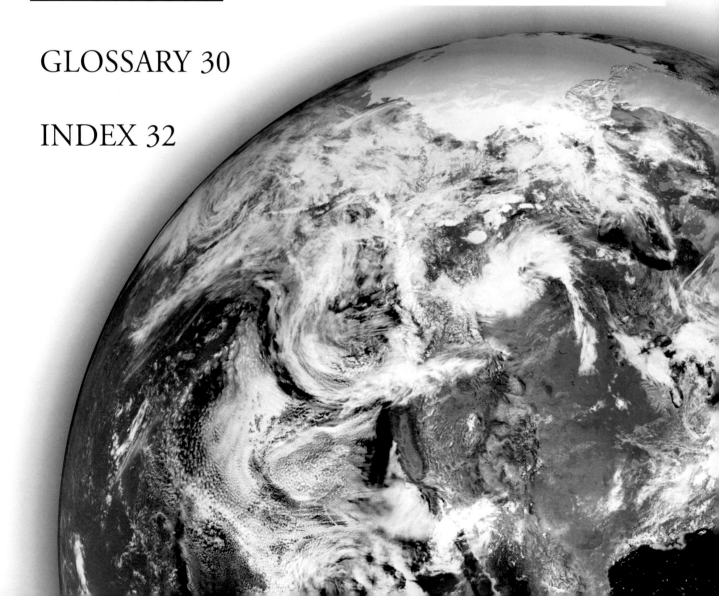

FRUIT
Fruit, like all plant resources, draws energy from the Sun.

FISH
Fish are among the many resources found in Earth's seas.

WATER
People, animals and plants need water to survive.

WIND POWER
Like water and the Sun, wind is a renewable resource and can be used to generate electricity.

CHAPTER 1:
Earth's Natural Resources

Look around you. Everything in your daily life – your toothbrush, the food for your lunch, the clothes you wear, the heat in your home – can be traced back to Earth's natural resources. Natural resources are the materials and sources of energy that come from our planet.

GIFTS THAT KEEP ON GIVING

As their name tells us, Earth's resources all come from nature. They include water, plant and animal life, coal, oil, minerals, and energy from wind and the Sun. People all over the world depend on Earth's natural

THE BLUE PLANET

About 70% of Earth's surface is made up of water.

All the water on Earth today has been here since our planet was formed billions of years ago! And, as far as anyone knows, it is all the water that will ever be on Earth. About 97 percent of Earth's water is salt water in the oceans. Less than 3 percent is fresh water. Much of Earth's fresh water is frozen in ice. It is in the glaciers of the Arctic, the Antarctic, and mountains around the world. Water is considered a renewable resource. It is renewed through the water cycle.

resources for their survival. We also depend on them to provide everything that helps make our lives more comfortable, interesting, and enjoyable. But it is up to us to take care of these resources. We need to be sure that they will be around for many generations.

Even a small area of land contains many natural resources. What resources do you see in this picture?

A WEALTH OF RESOURCES

SOIL
Rich soil is a resource farmers work hard to protect. Many of today's farmers have learned ways to fight erosion and keep the soil healthy – while still getting a good crop.

DIAMONDS
Diamonds are among the minerals called gemstones. Like other minerals, they occur naturally. People value diamonds and other gems because they are so beautiful and difficult to find.

ALMOST ANYTHING IMAGINABLE
Everything these moviegoers are enjoying has its origins in natural resources. The fabric and metal in the seats come from cotton and iron ore. The popcorn comes from fields of corn. Even the film in the projector is made from petroleum!

DEFINING NATURAL RESOURCES

Natural resources may be grouped in several ways. One way is to list them as either renewable or nonrenewable. Renewable resources are those that nature can replace, recycle, or regrow in a short time. Animals, plants, water, Sun energy, and wind energy are examples of renewable resources. But remember: even renewable resources can be used up if we waste them.

Fish from oceans, rivers, and lakes are renewable resources. However, overfishing is threatening the survival of some types of fish, such as the tuna that have been caught in this picture.

Most trees are said to be renewable. But replacing an old redwood tree – known as old growth – can take hundreds of years. So old-growth trees are called nonrenewable.

Other resources are nonrenewable. This means that nature needs millions of years to create them. Examples of nonrenewable resources include oil, coal, natural gas, gold, silver, platinum, and other minerals. Today, people are using up these resources more quickly than nature can replenish them. When our supply of nonrenewable resources runs out, there won't be more.

LOSING RESOURCES

THE QUAGGA: EXTINCT

Thousands of quagga once grazed on the plains of southern Africa, but they were hunted to extinction in the wild in about 1870. The last quagga in captivity died in a zoo in Amsterdam in 1883.

HAWAIIAN BIRDS THREATENED

The mongoose was brought to Hawaii in 1883 to help control the islands' rat population. However, mongooses began eating bird eggs, thereby threatening Hawaii's ground-nesting birds.

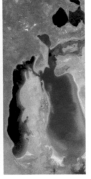

THE ARAL SEA: THREATENED

The Aral Sea sits on the border between Khazakstan and Uzbekistan. Over the last 30 years, this sea has lost 60 percent of its water volume. Since the 1960s, its water sources have been used for irrigation. These satellite images show the sea in August 1989 (left) and August 2003.

SOIL – WHAT KIND OF RESOURCE IS IT?

Some natural resources are not easy to list as either renewable or nonrenewable. Soil is one example. Although many people consider soil nonrenewable, it can be renewed. But it takes many, many years. Nature may need thousands of years to make a few centimetres of healthy, mineral-rich soil.

*Iron ore is an inorganic resource.
Here it is heated to create steel in a
process called smelting. The large, hot, orange
steel sheet is being rolled by a machine in a steel mill.*

ORGANIC RESOURCES

Natural resources can also be grouped as either organic or
inorganic. Organic resources come from things that are or were
once alive. These include plants and animals. Think about all
of the ways to use organic resources in a day. You might wear
clothes made out of cotton or lamb's wool. Lunch might be a
cheese sandwich and an apple. Your school work is written on
paper, maybe at a desk – both of which are made out of wood.

INORGANIC RESOURCES

Other natural resources are inorganic. Inorganic resources
do not come from living organisms. Minerals and rocks are

SKYSCRAPING RESOURCES

The Sears Tower in Chicago, USA, is North
America's tallest building. It stands 442
metres and 110 stories tall. It was built
with 68,946 tonnes of steel which is made
from the natural resource of iron ore.

examples of inorganic materials. Our daily lives are filled with examples of these resources, too. The fizzy drink can you recycled today is made from aluminium. Your mother's earrings have opals in them. The building site crew down the street is using steel in the buildings being put up.

As a renewable organic resource, trees are often grown in order to be harvested, just like many other plants. Whole forests may be grown (above left) specifically to be cut down for the wood they produce. Meanwhile the careful cultivating of new crops of trees (above right) assures that these resources stay renewable.

WOOL – AN ORGANIC RESOURCE

Wool is only one product that sheep provide us with. We also eat their meat (as lamb or mutton) and make cheeses (such as feta cheese) and yogurt from their milk.

Sheep produce a fleece.   **The sheep is sheared.**

The fleece is spun into wool.   **Wool is made into clothes and other textiles.**

ORGANIC OR INORGANIC?

In simple terms, organic means anything that comes from a plant or an animal. Inorganic describes anything that was never living.

Examine the following list and decide whether the item listed comes from an organic or inorganic resource.

1 Drinking glass
2 Honey
3 Icicle
4 Cooking oil made from corn or sunflowers
5 Leather ball
6 Mobile phone
7 Spaghetti sauce
8 Baseball bat

What other items can you add to this list to stump others?

ANSWERS: 1. Inorganic 2. Organic 3. Inorganic 4. Organic 5. Organic 6. Inorganic 7. Organic 8. Organic

Natural gas forms along with oil. Early oil drillers considered it worthless. They burned it just to get rid of it! Some countries do that even today.

CHAPTER 2:
Nonrenewable Resources

Nonrenewable resources are found on Earth in limited amounts. This means that they cannot be replaced easily. At least, that is, they cannot be replaced as quickly as many of them are being used. And people have been using some of them at an increasing rate for years.

FOSSIL FUELS

Many nonrenewable resources are fossil fuels. Among these are oil, natural gas, and coal. They are called fossil fuels because they were made from the decaying remains of animals, plants, and other organisms.

These materials have been forming in Earth's crust (the outermost solid layer of the Earth) for millions of years. Some of this matter fell to the ocean floor and was covered over by sediment. Some of the matter was buried deep in the ground. In either case,

These rigs (right) drill for oil around the clock. We use this oil in our cars and to heat our homes. The oil was formed from organisms that lived in water millions of years ago. Oil deposits found today might once have been covered by oceans or seas.

DRILLING FOR OIL

The first oil well was drilled in Titusville, Pennsylvania, USA, in 1859. There, a retired railroad conductor named Edwin Drake struck oil on his farm. People were first interested in oil for use in kerosene lamps. Use for cars and heating came later. But Drake's discovery still began the modern oil industry. His well was the first drilled just for the purpose of finding oil.

the decay was covered over by layer after layer of other materials. It all became part of Earth's crust. There it sat for millions of years, compressed beneath the heat and weight of the matter covering it. Slowly the material formed fossil fuels.

FOSSIL FUELS: WORLD CONSUMPTION 1965 - 2005

As this chart shows, the consumption of fossil fuels (coal, gas, and oil) doubled as a group between the 1960s and 2005. Less dramatic, however, was the rise of oil as a source of energy, especially compared to coal and natural gas. Note the use of two renewable resources: hydroelectric power and nuclear energy.

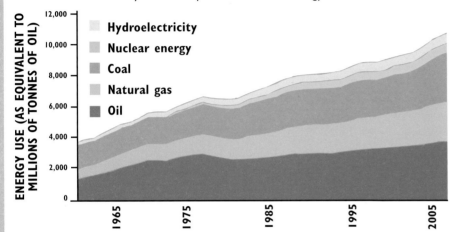

ENERGY USE (AS EQUIVALENT TO MILLIONS OF TONNES OF OIL)

- Hydroelectricity
- Nuclear energy
- Coal
- Natural gas
- Oil

12,000 / 10,000 / 8,000 / 6,000 / 4,000 / 2,000 / 0

1965 1975 1985 1995 2005

HOW COAL IS FORMED

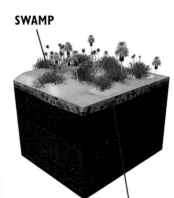

SWAMP

PLANT DEBRIS

About 300 million years ago, tree-filled swamps covered much of the Earth. As plants and trees died, they settled to the bottom of these swamps. There, this matter began to decay.

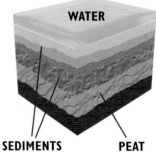

WATER

SEDIMENTS   PEAT

The decaying matter formed peat. This spongy material was soon buried under more layers.

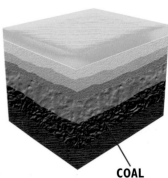

COAL

After millions of years of pressure and heat, the peat became coal.

USING FOSSIL FUELS

Roughly 80 percent of the energy used worldwide comes from fossil fuels. Most of these fossil fuels, such as oil, natural gas, and coal, must be changed, or converted, in some way to create energy that we can reuse. Today, through technology, we are able to convert fossil fuels to usable energy more and more efficiently.

Oil and natural gas are very much in demand as energy sources today. And no wonder! They power our vehicles. They heat our homes and businesses. They are also used to make plastics, medicines, cosmetics, synthetic fabrics, and many other products.

Oil is used in the production of items we might not ever imagine it to be, such as ink for printing money, asphalt for roads, lipstick, and even trainers.

A LOOK AT HOW FOSSIL FUELS ARE USED (BY RANK)

FOSSIL FUEL	MAJOR PRODUCERS	USE OF FOSSIL FUEL
Oil	Saudi Arabia, Russia, USA	• As petrol, diesel fuel, jet fuel to power cars, buses, trains, and planes • Heating oil • In the manufacturing of plastics, synthetic clothing (such as nylon, polyester, kevlar), cosmetics, medicines, fertilisers, insecticides,etc.
Coal	China, USA, India	• Fuel for heat, light, and generating electricity
Natural Gas	USA, Russia, Canada	• Fuel for lighting, heating, cooking, manufacturing, and generating electricity

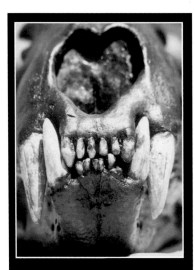

LA BREA: TREASURE TROVE OF DEATH

Tar pits form when crude oil from Earth's crust seeps up to the surface through cracks in the crust. The La Brea Tar Pits in Los Angeles, USA, are famous for their collection of fossilised animals and plants from the Pleistocene Period. The remains of insects, reptiles, amphibians, birds, fish, and even mammals, such as sabre-toothed tigers (as above), have been discovered.

THE POLITICS OF OIL

Today, uses for oil continue to rise. Quantities of it, however, continue to decrease.

Many nations have large supplies of oil beneath their land. Others need that oil for their own use. One-third of the largest oil-supplying nations are in the Middle East. The nations that use the most oil are the United States, China, Japan, and many industrialised nations in Europe and North America. These factors affect the balance between the world's oil supply and the demand for oil. They also affect the economies and politics of the West and the Middle East.

This container ship is powered by diesel or another oil-based fuel. Much of its cargo consists of oil-based products. The containers holding the cargo are made of oil-based materials. And the hold of this ship is probably carrying oil which will power other means of transport.

In large urban settings such as Los Angeles (right), burning fossil fuels causes air pollution. Exhaust from cars, trucks, and other vehicles is a major contributor.

PROBLEMS WITH FOSSIL FUEL RESERVES

Humans have found many uses for coal, natural gas, and oil. But using these fossil fuels also has its problems. The biggest is pollution. Most fossil fuels must be burned to be used. Burning them releases their energy. Only then do they create heat, produce electricity, or otherwise perform as we need them to. As they burn, however, they also release the following harmful substances into the atmosphere:

- **Carbon monoxide:** This adds to urban smog, air pollution, and global warming.

- **Sulphur dioxide:** This comes from coal and causes acid rain.

- **Release particulates:** These small bits of matter are released by burning fuel and are not healthy for people to breathe.

MAJOR AIR POLLUTANTS AND THEIR SOURCES

These two charts show some of Earth's major air pollutants (below left) and the sources of these pollutants (below right). The percentage of pollutants in the atmosphere as a whole may be a tiny fraction of one percent. But this tiny amount can still be very harmful. The pollutants chart (below left) shows how the pollution in our atmosphere is broken down between different pollutants.

POLLUTANTS CHART

Nitrogen oxides (produced by burning fossil fuels) 14.8%

Carbon monoxide 49.1%

Volatile organics (chemicals released by paint, glue, and other products) 16.4%

Particulates

Sulphur dioxide

CAUSES CHART

Miscellaneous

Factories and refineries 15%

Incineration of waste; odour from landfill 2.5%

9%

Transportation: cars, trucks, planes 46.2%

27.3%

Fuel combustion: steam generators in power plants

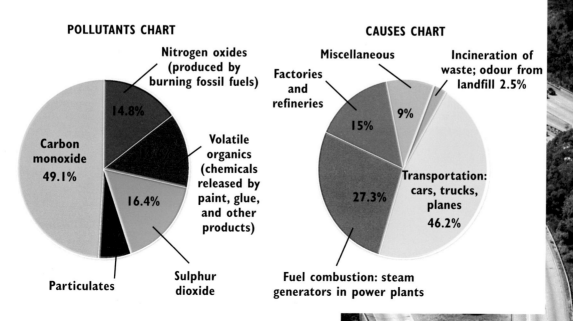

Underground mines put miners in danger of mine collapse and lung disease from breathing coal dust. But strip mining (above) can scar the land as the topsoil is stripped away to get at the coal beneath.

A RISKY BUSINESS

Aside from the pollution, getting to these fossil fuels is difficult. They are often buried deep in the earth – right where they formed. They must be brought to the surface by mining, drilling, piping, or other means. These methods can be harmful to both the planet and the people who collect them.

OIL SPILLS

Oil spills are a danger whenever crude oil must be transported. Spills can kill animals and destroy whole ecosystems. They can also harm communities and industries along the coasts. In 1979, the tanker *Atlantic Empress* collided with the tanker *Aegean Captain*. The two ships spilled 276,000 tonnes of oil into the Caribbean Sea. This is the worst oil tanker spill on record.

NOT JUST YOUR MOTHER'S JEWELLERY

Many diamonds come from Africa. But Russia, Canada, Australia, and Brazil are also big suppliers of diamonds. Mining diamonds can be brutal, dangerous work. Once mined, diamonds have many uses. As a rare and precious mineral, they are cut and polished to become expensive jewellery. As the hardest mineral known, diamonds are used in industry for grinding, polishing, and cutting machine parts and other hard substances – including other diamonds!

MINERALS AND ROCK RESOURCES

Minerals and rocks are also nonrenewable resources. They make up Earth's crust and other solid parts of our planet.

A HUGE AND VARIED RESOURCE

Scientists have identified 3,800 different minerals. Some, such as ores, contain metals. The metals can be stripped out and used in building and in manufacturing. They are especially useful in electrical supplies. Metal is a good conductor of heat and electricity. Other rare minerals, like rubies and emeralds, are often used in jewellery. Precious metals like gold, silver, and platinum may also be used in jewellery.

Like this piece of quartz, a specific mineral always has the same makeup – and therefore has a very definite look.

Like any other mineral, salt must be taken from the earth. Here, workers gather halite (the scientific name for salt) from the Colchani Salt Pans in Bolivia. The salt pans are large plains made entirely of the salt that will eventually be used to season our food.

METALS: A USEFUL RESOURCE

Metals are often extracted from other resources, such as minerals. Once mined, a metal can be combined with other substances to produce an alloy.

NICKEL
Nickel is used mostly as an alloy. Combined with iron, it gives great strength to steel. The nickel used in coins is actually an alloy made up mostly of copper.

TUNGSTEN
Tungsten melts at 3,410° C, making it the most heat-resistant metal known. It is used as the wire filament in light bulbs.

ALUMINIUM
Aluminium is lightweight yet strong. It can be shaped easily when heated and stays tough under extreme cold. Aluminium is one of the most useful metals known. It is used for foil, cans, and in building materials.

A STABLE AND RELIABLE RESOURCE

The term mineral is often used for anything nonliving taken from the ground. But it actually refers to specific substances. True minerals have set chemical makeups. A mineral will be the same no matter where it is found. This is not true of rocks. Samples of the same type of rock may have very different chemical makeups.

THE PROPERTIES OF MINERALS: A SHORT GLOSSARY

Some common properties of minerals include the following:

Colour: a mineral's true colour.

Hardness: this is measured on a scale of hardness devised by German geologist Friedrich Mohs.

Cleavage: the way a mineral breaks along its planes in parallel lines and creates a smooth surface. Mica is known for this.

Fracture: the way a mineral separates if it does not break along its planes.

Specific gravity: a mineral's weight compared to an equal volume of water.

Lustre: the way a mineral reflects light.

Crystal form: the arrangement of a mineral's atoms. Amethyst's crystal form shows in angular shapes on its surface.

COPPER

MICA

AMETHYST

CHAPTER 3:
Renewable Resources

Earth's renewable resources are those that can be replaced in a short amount of time. Energy from the Sun, water, wind, animals and plants are all renewable resources.

SMART AND NECESSARY

Even the air we breathe and heat produced inside the Earth are resources. Water, sunlight and plants are crucial to life on the planet. So taking care of Earth's renewable resources isn't just smart – it is necessary.

ECOSYSTEMS: RENEWABLE RESOURCES AT WORK

An ecosystem is a community in nature. It is any place where plants and animals depend on each other for food. Within that ecosystem the animals and plants are a renewable resource. The animals and plants also depend on other renewable resources, such as water and the Sun, to exist in their ecosystem.

Water. Air. Wind. Sun. We live every day with a number of renewable resources at our fingertips. Earth has more renewable than nonrenewable resources.

In a garden, plants rely on the soil and atmosphere for water and carbon dioxide. They also use energy from sunlight to convert the carbon dioxide and water into food (carbohydrates). Honeybees, birds, and other animals eat the plants or drink their nectar. In turn, these animals carry pollen from one plant to another. This helps the plants to reproduce.

Meat-eating animals eat plant-eating animals. The nutrition produced by plants then enters the meat-eaters' bodies.

When plants, insects, and other organisms die, their decaying remains add nutrients to the soil. This provides nourishment to worms and insects.

HELPING ECOSYSTEMS HELP THEMSELVES

By monitoring the condition of Earth's ecosystems, we can help nature maintain a balance among the many renewable resources that keep an ecosystem healthy.

CUTTING DOWN WITH CARE
Forests can stay renewable as long as people help forests replenish their own supply of trees. Planned and controlled logging keeps forests free of sick or dying trees.

MANAGING ANIMAL NUMBERS
Control of animal populations assures food for all. Too many fish in one place can choke off their food supply. Overfishing can deprive water resources of their balance between plant and animal life.

WATER FOR ALL
Dams control the flow of water and create lakes and reservoirs. These provide a source of drinking water and recreation for humans and drinking water and habitats for wildlife.

THE WATER CYCLE

The Sun drives the water cycle that moves water around our Earth.

2. The warm gas rises in the air, where it cools and forms tiny droplets. This is called condensation.

3. As the drops get heavier, they fall as rain or snow. This is called precipitation.

1. The Sun warms the sea's surface, causing the water to turn into vapour. This is called evaporation.

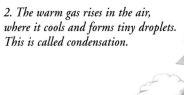

4. Rivers carry the rainwater back to the sea. This is called accumulation.

ALTERNATE ENERGY SOURCES

Solar energy. Wind energy. Hydroelectric power. Geothermal power.
Tidal power. Alternate energy sources offer some exciting possibilities
both for now and into the future.

Some of these energy sources – like solar, wind, and hydroelectric power – have
been tested. All of them have found some use and success. But for all of these
sources, even if taken together as a group, their use is still small compared to our
total energy consumption.

*Heated water from the
Svartsengi Geothermal Power
Plant in Grindavik, Iceland,
flows to a famous health spa
called Blue Lagoon.*

GEOTHERMAL POWER

Geothermal power comes from using the heat of the Earth itself.
This heat, in the form of hot water and steam, is often found in areas of volcanic
activity. With pipes and pumps, the water or
steam is taken from underground reservoirs.
It is used to power turbines that then
generate electricity.

TIDAL POWER

Like hydroelectric power, tidal power also uses energy from water. In this case,
the energy is generated by the tides that advance and recede in the oceans and
large lakes. Dams stretching over bays capture water at high tide.
Later, as water is released with the outgoing
tide, the movement powers turbines and
generates electricity.

WIND POWER

Wind power is created by harnessing the power of the wind. In the past, people used windmills. Today they use powerful wind turbines. Both capture the energy from the wind, using it to turn the blades at the top of a tower. Today, a wind turbine's turning blades are used to generate electricity.

Wind power is renewable, and it doesn't pollute. But some people think a hillside dotted with giant wind turbines, as seen here in the Mojave Desert in the US, is an eyesore and makes too much noise.

ALTERNATE ENERGIES AT WORK

SOLAR POWER

Solar power comes from the Sun. Energy from the Sun is collected by capturing its rays in special solar panels. This energy is converted to electricity, which then becomes an energy source for running all of a building's appliances, including sources of heating and cooling. In the picture above, a parking metre is powered by a solar panel.

SOLAR-POWERED SUN TEA

The Sun's energy is there for the taking. Test that idea by making yourself some Sun tea. Even a slightly gray day will give you enough power from the Sun to provide the energy needed for water to heat up and brew a large container of tea.

Materials needed
- A large clear jug/container (with cover)
- Cold water
- 2–6 tea bags, depending on the size of the container
- Glasses, lots of ice, lemon, and sugar or an artificial sweetener

1) Fill your container with water. Add the tea bags. Place the container in a sunny place. Allow tea to brew in the sunlight. This may take several hours.

2) When the tea has brewed to a dark colour, remove the tea bags. Be sure to refrigerate your Sun tea as soon as it's brewed. Cool your tea in the refrigerator, or add plenty of ice, lemon, or sugar or sweetener and drink immediately. Enjoy your solar-powered iced tea!

HYDROELECTRIC POWER

Hydroelectric power is generated by moving water. Power plants built over flowing rivers convert the water's energy into electrical energy. First the water is stored behind a dam. As the water is released, the movement turns huge turbine blades. This, in turn, generates electricity.

THE OXYGEN CYCLE

Plants absorb carbon dioxide and water. They convert them into carbohydrates and oxygen during photosynthesis.

Photosynthesis is the process by which plants use sunlight to produce their own energy.

Plants absorb carbon dioxide and give off oxygen.

Animals and people breathe in the oxygen and breathe out carbon dioxide.

PLANT RESOURCES

It would be easy to overlook plants as valuable natural resources. They are so much a part of our lives. As part of the oxygen cycle, plants play a key role in renewing the oxygen in Earth's atmosphere. Without plants, humans and animals would not have oxygen to breathe.

Plants are also a food resource in all of Earth's ecosystems. For humans in particular, plants are a food source whether growing wild or as crops that we plant and harvest.

RAINFOREST TREASURE

Many scientists think that about two-thirds of all plant species in the world are found in rainforests. These plants produce as much as 40 percent of Earth's oxygen. Rainforest plants have given us hundreds of varieties of fruits, vegetables, spices, and coffee. The raw materials for many products, from chewing gum to rubber, come from rainforest trees.

MEDICINE CABINET TO THE WORLD

Scientists estimate that plants from the rainforest have provided the basis for about 25 percent of the world's medicines. From compounds that help heal wounds to drugs that fight cancer, especially leukemia and other childhood cancers: Earth's rainforests could hold the promise for future success in treating illness and disease.

Warm, wet rainforests—like this one in Madagascar—have more kinds of trees than anywhere else on Earth. Protecting rainforests also means protecting countless plant and animal species.

BIOMES – MAPPING EARTH'S NATURAL RESOURCES

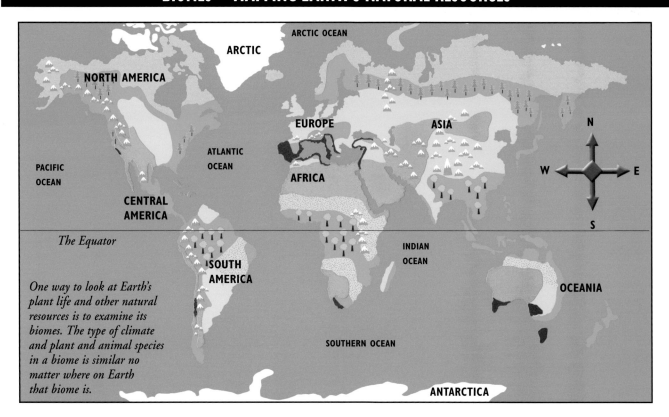

ARCTIC OCEAN

ARCTIC

NORTH AMERICA

EUROPE

ASIA

ATLANTIC OCEAN

PACIFIC OCEAN

AFRICA

CENTRAL AMERICA

N
W E
S

The Equator

INDIAN OCEAN

SOUTH AMERICA

OCEANIA

One way to look at Earth's plant life and other natural resources is to examine its biomes. The type of climate and plant and animal species in a biome is similar no matter where on Earth that biome is.

SOUTHERN OCEAN

ANTARCTICA

TEMPERATE GRASSLANDS
Warm, dry summers, cool or cold winters; rainfall supports lots of plant and animal life

TUNDRA
Cold, windy plains; soil freezes just below surface; plants need short roots to absorb nutrients

CHAPARRAL
Flat plains, rocky hills, mountain slopes; plants and animals adapted to hot, dry summers, mild winters

 SAVANNA
Large plains with scattered trees and bushes; amount of foliage determined by extent of rainfall

ARCTIC/ANTARCTICA
Cold and dry all year; frozen ground and icy seas; animals live off rich marine life

TEMPERATE DECIDUOUS FOREST
Plants bloom and thrive in summer, and are usually dormant in winter

 CONIFEROUS FOREST
Cold evergreen forest; most animals migrate or hibernate in winter

 TROPICAL RAINFOREST
Hot, wet climate, with lots of sun and rain supporting huge variety of life

 DESERT
Dry land, little rain; wide variety of plants, including cacti that store water

OCEAN
Major component of water cycle; saltwater environment supports enormous variety of marine life

PAPER OR FORESTS?

It's no secret that Earth's rainforests are in danger. It has been estimated that about 315 thousand square kilometres of rainforest is cut down every year for logging and to create farmland. Most of the logging industry is based on the demand for wood and paper products. About 95 percent of all paper is made from wood, but now paper can be efficiently and successfully reused through recycling. Think of how much rainforest could be saved just from recycling the daily newspaper!*

* See the newspaper recycling experiment on page 29.

ANIMALS AT WORK

PACK ANIMALS

Some animals have many uses. Llamas, like camels, horses, and even elephants, are called pack animals. This means they are used to carry things. Llamas also have hair that makes a useful fibre.

AQUACULTURE

Some fish, such as salmon and trout, are both caught in the wild and farmed. Fish farming is known as aquaculture. As world supplies in the wild have declined, fish farming has grown. According to recent figures, 43 percent of all eaten fish come from farms.

WHOSE RESOURCE?

The North American Northern Spotted Owl prefers nesting in old-growth forests. Old-growth forests have lots of undergrowth and decaying trees. The owl has become the focus of a debate between environmental groups and companies that log these forests for their ancient and highly valuable trees.

ANIMAL RESOURCES

Just like plants, animals are a renewable resource. In thinking about animals as a resource, you might first think of them as sources of food or other products for people. Fish, for example, feed people all over the world. Sheep, goats, and cattle give milk and meat. Hides from many animals have value when building shelters or as clothing and shoes.

Animals also have a major effect on the environment. Each animal helps balance the ecosystem it is part of. Small fish feed people. They also feed sharks in the ocean. Coyotes have been known to kill sheep and sometimes get

Some animals, such as cattle, are such important resources that humans have domesticated, or tamed, them. Herds of cattle are kept all over the world.

into rubbish in urban areas. But they also control the rodent population around farms and towns. Each of these animals plays an important role in its own ecosystem.

THE BIG PICTURE

Each individual ecosystem contributes to the health of our planet, which is a collection of ecosystems. Sometimes, however, humans exploit the resources in one ecosystem. We cut down too many trees in a rainforest or damage the landscape while mining for coal. We have to think about the effect this might have on the planet as a whole.

GO WILD WHERE YOU LIVE!

Exploring the wildlife where you live gives you a chance to see nature up close, and may lead to some surprise discoveries! Try the following activities to learn more about the wildlife and natural resources near your home.

1) Using online sources, the library, or visits to a local zoo or nature centre, find out what kinds of wildlife live in your area.

2) Be an observer of life around you! Keep track of the kinds of animal life you actually see near where you live. Write down what you observe in a notebook for one week.

3) Also observe what resources in your local area these animals rely on to survive. Are the resources organic or inorganic? Are they natural or made by humans?

4) Can you identify some ways in which the animals' resources might be threatened? For example, are homes or industrial buildings being built on wild areas that are an animal's habitat? Is a river in your area becoming polluted by litter?

THE AMERICAN BISON

In the 1800s, bison populations on the Great Plains of North America may have been as great as 30 to 75 million. Native Americans relied on the bison for food, clothing, and fuel. Non-Native settlers hunted the bison aggressively – often just for sport. They nearly drove it to extinction. By the 1880s, the bison population may have been as low as 1,000. The government and conservationists worked to protect the bison, and its population has grown again. But it will never reach the huge numbers it once had.

WATER USE IN THE HOME

Here are some common uses of water in the home. Also shown is the average amount of water each activity uses .

• One bath: 80 litres

• One shower: 35 litres

• One toilet flush: 8 litres

•One dishwasher load: 25 litres

• One washing machine load: 65 litres

In an average home which activity do you think uses the most water per day?

Answer: flushing the toilet

CHAPTER 4:
Conservation – What Can You Do?

Taking care of our natural resources will help ensure that future generations have what they need to survive on our planet. It will also teach us to become responsible caretakers of the world we call home.

REDUCE

You may have heard the expression 'Reduce, Reuse, Recycle.' Those who are concerned about the future of our planet feel that we must become better at reducing our need for natural resources.

The more we know about our interaction with Earth and its natural resources, the better off we will be.

One of the most important ways that we can cut back our use of natural resources is to use less oil. This will help conserve fossil fuels, a nonrenewable source of energy. It will also reduce the release of pollutants into the atmosphere. Many cities are looking into providing 'clean' public transport. In future you might ride on buses and trains powered by electricity, solar power, or other renewable forms of energy.

Often, reducing energy consumption can also improve our health. Riding a bike or walking instead of driving can benefit both the planet and you.

HOW MUCH DO YOU USE?

How much of a resource do you use? Try this experiment to figure out how much water you might use washing your hands in a year.

Materials needed
- Large bowl
- Container with measuring marks

1) Wash your hands as normal, but place a large bowl in your sink to catch the water you use. Pour the used water into a measuring cup. How much have you used? Record the amount in a notebook.

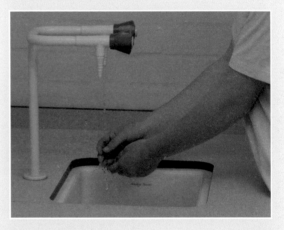

2) Keep track of how many times you wash your hands in a day. Multiply the amount of water you used in your first hand washing by the number of times a day you washed.

3) Multiply the amount of water you use in one day by 365. This number should show roughly how much water you use just washing your hands in a year. Did that total surprise you?

TAKING IT EASY WITH ENERGY

PLANNING FOR THE FUTURE
Some energy-saving solutions, like putting solar panels on a home, are more expensive to start with. But in the long run they will reduce our need for fossil fuels to provide homes and businesses with heat and other energy.

EVERY LITTLE BIT COUNTS
Your local electricity or water company offers many good ideas for conserving energy. Your family can install low-flowing showerheads and toilets. You can turn down the thermostat in the winter – and wear a jumper!

EARTHWORM COMPOSTERS

Some people use earthworm boxes as a way to compost. Earthworm boxes are made of wood or plastic and filled with shredded newspaper or cardboard and decaying leaves. A handful of soil should also be added. Soil is gritty and helps worms break down food particles. Boxes can be made at home or bought from garden supply stores.

In the box, the earthworms are fed kitchen scraps such as fruit and vegetable peelings, bread and egg shells. (Do not add meat scraps.) The worms eat this matter, which otherwise goes into landfills. Under ideal conditions each earthworm eats its own weight in waste every 24 hours.

The worms' droppings mix with the dirt in the box to make rich, nutrient-filled compost that can be used in the garden to feed plants or even to grow more vegetables!

REUSE

In addition to reducing our need for resources, reusing and recycling are two ways we can all play a role in conserving energy. Reusing allows us to make a second (or third or fourth) use of an existing object. Think about that box that brought a package to your door. Or the shopping bag you carried into the kitchen. Most items that we use to carry or send things in can be reused over and over.

RECYCLE

Recycling allows us to make new things out of used materials. Many materials can be recycled, such as paper, plastic, metal, and glass. Many of these materials are already part of recycling programs.

Most communities have recycling programs that allow us all to easily dispose of metal cans, drinks bottles, and newspapers. These programs give us a chance to enjoy the good feeling we all get when we know we have helped conserve our planet's resources.

This is paper collected from recycling points waiting to be processed and recycled.

Recycling products from home is one of the easiest ways to get involved in conservation efforts. Anyone can recycle!

MAKE RECYCLED PAPER

The newspapers and scrap paper you take to the recycling centre is turned into pulp and then into new recycled paper. You can try making your own recycled paper at home or in your classroom.

Materials needed
- Large square or rectangular baking tray
- A wash basin or mixing bowl
- 3 cups of water
- A newspaper
- A rolling pin

1) Tear one to two pages of newspaper into small pieces of 2.5 cm or less.

2) Put some of the paper pieces into a large bowl and add all the water. Keep adding paper. Tear and squeeze the paper until you get a mush that looks like thick porridge.

3) Turn the baking tray upside down and put about 1 cup of the paper pulp over the bottom of the baking tray. Spread the pulp evenly over the baking tray with your fingers.

4) Lay several sheets of newspaper over the pulp to hold it onto the baking tray. Carefully turn the baking tray over and remove the baking tray. Your pulp layer is now sitting on the newspaper.

5) Fold the newspaper over the pulp. Roll the rolling pin over the newspaper parcel to blot out the extra water.

6) Uncover the pulp and let the sheet of new 'paper' dry completely!

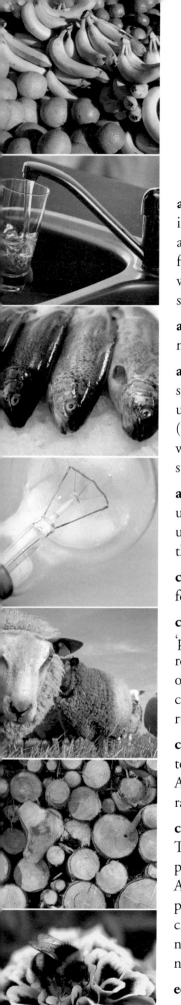

GLOSSARY

acid rain Air pollution mixed with water in the atmosphere that then falls to Earth as rain. Acid rain contains pollution in the form of acids. It can dirty the soil and water, harm plants, and even damage hard surfaces such as stone.

alloy A substance made by combining metal with another material.

atmosphere The thick layer of air that surrounds the Earth. The gases that make up the Earth's atmosphere include nitrogen (78%) and oxygen (21%). There is also water, and small quantities of other gases such as argon and carbon dioxide.

atom All materials and subtances are made up of atoms. They are the smallest possible unit of an element that still behaves like that element.

carbon monoxide A poisonous gas formed in the burning of fossil fuels.

conservation This word means the 'planned management of natural resources'. In our everyday lives it means only using what we need. For example, we can conserve water by not leaving the tap running when we brush our teeth.

conservationist A person who works to protect Earth's natural resources. A conservationist may work to save rainforests and stop them being cut down.

crude oil The natural state of petroleum. This fossil fuel formed from decaying plants, animals, and other organisms. As crude oil comes from the ground, it is piped or shipped to a refinery. There, the crude oil is refined. It is used to produce a number of different fuels, including natural gas, petrol, kerosene, and more.

economy A system of exchange of goods and services.

ecosystem An ecosystem is a community in which animals and plants rely on each other and on resources such as water and sunlight. An ecosystem can be large like a woodland, or small, like a single tree.

element A substance made up of only one type of atom. Elements cannot be broken down into other substances.

erosion When land or rocks are worn away by the force of wind or rain.

extinct When an animal or plant no longer exists on Earth.

fossils Remains or imprints of ancient plants and animals that have been preserved in rocks.

fresh water Water sources, such as most rivers and lakes, that do not contain salt.

gemstones Precious rocks and minerals, such as rubies, emeralds, and pearls. They are often used in jewellery.

generation The lifespan of a group of living things, such as plants or animals. A generation is usually counted as being the period of time between the birth of a parent and the birth of their young.

geothermal power Energy, such as electricity, that is created by harnessing heat from within the Earth. Hot magma under the Earth's crust heats up water on the surface. Steam from the hot water is used to drive turbines in power stations.

global warming A gradual warming of the Earth's atmosphere. Most scientists believe that this is caused by humans burning fossils fuels, such as oil and coal. The burning of these fuels gives off gases that trap too much of the Sun's heat in the Earth's atmosphere.

habitat An environment in which a particular plant or animal does best and is most likely found.

hydroelectric power Electricity produced by power plants that use the energy created by moving water.

inorganic Something that is not living, such as metal or rock.

irrigation The process of bringing water to a place. For example pumping water from a river to irrigate (water) crops.

kerosene A thin, light oil used in lamps and heaters and for cleaning.

minerals Solid, usually inorganic, substances that occur naturally on Earth, such as gold, copper, iron and salt.

natural resources The materials, energy sources and living things found in nature that are useful to people and other living creatures. Water, air, minerals, the Sun's energy, plants and animals are all natural resources.

nitrogen oxides Gases produced in the burning of fossil fuels. Nitrogen oxides are one of the gases that contribute to acid rain.

nonrenewable Unable to be renewed. Fossil fuels and minerals, such as gemstones, are part of this group.

nuclear energy Energy stored in the nucleus, or core, of the atom. This energy is harnessed by releasing it from the atom. It can then be used to make electricity.

ore A rock or mineral containing metal that can be extracted (removed). Ores are mined for the metals they contain.

organic Something that is living, such as an animal or plant.

organism A living being.

overfishing Catching too many of a specific type of fish so that the population of that fish does not have time to breed and renew itself. Eventually overfishing of some fish species could lead to extinction.

particulates Small bits of substances,

such as dirt and aerosol droplets, and other pollutants.

peat A brown material made from decayed plants, which is found in marshy places.

petroleum The substance, created by decaying plant and animal remains, from which oil, gas, and other products come.

politics A system of policies and practices influencing actions of a group of people.

pollinate To transfer pollen from one plant to another, in preparation for plant reproduction.

recede To move back.

renewable Able to be renewed. Plants and animals are renewable resources.

salt water Water, such as ocean water, that contains dissolved salts.

sediments Tiny grains of materials, such as rock and sand.

smog A foglike haze caused by pollution in the air. The word is formed by combining the words smoke and fog.

solar power Power created by harnessing the energy of the Sun as it reaches Earth.

sulphur oxide A gas that comes from the burning of fossil fuels and from natural occurrences such as volcanoes. It can be a major contributor to pollution.

tidal power Energy harnessed from the natural movement of bodies of water, such as oceans and lakes. Tidal power gets its energy from the natural rise and fall of the water at different times of the day.

volatile organics Chemicals, in the form of gases, that are released by products such as paint, glues and pesticides. They can cause pollution.

water cycle The constant movement of water from rivers, lakes, and the ocean up into the atmosphere and back down to Earth.

wind power Capturing the energy of the wind and using it to power windmills. The windmills drive turbines which produce electrical energy.